Bolumar
2010

TRUMP.ology

川語錄

We owe him [Trump] an open mind and the chance to lead.

我們虧欠他（川普）一個開闊的胸懷、以及一個機會讓他領導國家。

— Hillary Clinton / 希拉蕊 · 柯林頓

Chief Editor
編　　者

Chris Chang, DDS., PhD

張 慧 男　博士

Founder,   Beethoven Orthodontic Center and
             Newton's A, Inc.

Director,   Beethoven Effective Presentation Course

President,   International Association of Orthodontics
             and Implantology

PhD,   Indiana University-Purdue University
             Indianapolis, Orthodontics.

貝多芬齒顎矯正中心負責人
金牛頓藝術科技教育中心創辦人
貝多芬高效簡報法課程負責人
國際矯正植牙學會理事長
美國印第安那普渡大學齒顎矯正研究所博士

About Chief Editor
關 於 編 者

Born on December 25, 1961, Dr. Chris Chang, taught himself to become an expert "frog exterminator" as he grew up in the countryside of Taiwan. It took him 7 years, not the normal 6 years, to complete primary school; he was unable to communicate in Mandarin Chinese (only the local dialect) and had never worn a "proper" pair of shoes before graduation. Before pursuing his Ph.D. in the U.S., he had never spoken a word in English. Twenty years later on, he is invited to lecture locally and internationally on dentistry and professional presentation skills, as well as teaching domestic and global dental courses with his unique sense of humor, elegant slide design, dental expertise, and effective teaching methods. Since 1996, he has founded a number of dental clinics, providing orthodontic treatment, implant therapy, general dentistry and pedodontic care. Due to his passion for Steve Jobs and Apple's minimalistic design, he established Newton's A Technology Education Center, dedicated to the promotion of Apple's technology education and professional Keynote presentations.

張慧男，1961 年 12 月 25 日生。自幼在雲林鄉間成長，練就了一手殺青蛙的好本領。小學念了七年，畢業以前不會說國語，也沒有穿過布鞋。在 30 歲赴美攻讀博士之前不曾開口說過英文，二十年後以他獨特的幽默感、優美的幻燈片以及精湛的牙科技術和高效率的教學方法，經常受邀至台灣國內以及亞洲、歐美和中南美洲各國演講牙科與專業簡報等主題，並開設國內以及國際性的牙醫課程。除了自 1996 年開始陸續創立貝多芬牙醫集團旗下的矯正、植牙、一般牙科以及兒童牙科等診所之外，熱愛賈伯斯以及蘋果極簡式設計的他，於 2008 年創辦了金牛頓藝術科技教育中心，致力推廣蘋果相關的科技教育及 Keynote 專業簡報課程。

Content
目 錄

Introduction
導　　　言

It may seem strange way to start a book of Trump's quotes, but I'll do it anyway, with a quote from another man that I really respect, Warren Buffet; **"Stay where you are, you can achieve most of the job."**

Why have I started so? Well, the answer lies in this quote from Donald Trump:

"I rarely go out, because mostly, it's a waste of time." They sound pretty similar, don't they? Not only these two great businessmen share this theme, the late, great Steve Jobs also shared this perspective: **"If you are willing to travel around the world to meet a teacher, one will appear next door."**

Why Donald?

20 years ago, when I had returned from my Post-graduate studies in America, I was wanting to buy an office, to start off my own business. Having had no experience of real estate, I looked for advice from the best, whom I considered to be Donald Trump. I duly bought his book entitled "The Art of the Deal" and as I read it I began to feel myself being enlightened by his business acumen. As he started his campaign to become the President of the U.S., I dusted off this book and started to re-read it and then began to see just how my interest in him had developed. I believe it is not only studying his business experience that

is essential in understanding him, but also his lifestyle choices, as well as his words of course. I looked at his way of conducting himself from 3 different angles: firstly, the way he lives, his daily routine in particular, secondly, the way in which he conducts his business and thirdly, the way he talks.

As you may be aware, he lives in the biggest penthouse in New York City, hardly surprising, as he has such "big hands!!" He lives on the 66th, 67th and 68th floors, which must be a most remarkable place from which to view the Big Apple. His office is on the 26th floor, with a direct private elevator linking the two. The restaurant, in which he eats, is also located in the same Trump Tower. Therefore, most of his days are spent in his own building, allowing him to spend time on what he needs and his daily routine reflects the habits he has in order to have become a highly successful businessman.

Some of the ways he conducts his business are truly extraordinary and also systemized in priorities. First priority, the phone. Second priority, people can come to his office and thirdly, he (very rarely) goes to others. One of my favorite deals was the way he managed to buy Mar-a-Lago, when he had been told there was no way that it would be sold to him. It was donated to the government in 1973 to be used as a winter White House. However, In 1980, it was returned to the original owner's family as the annual US$1 million maintenance fees were too much. In came Trump, who with his street-wise business thinking managed to buy the resort for a very low price, having previously bought some of the land surrounding it. If any of you are interested in this, just google Mar-a-Lago and marvel at what he has changed it into. It is truly unbelievable! He is a real estate virtuoso!

This ability to not only think outside the box, but also perform outside the box really fascinates me and I feel this is one of his greatest assets. Again, similarities with Steve Jobs are abound and Trump openly shared his respect for Steve Jobs — "I've always been a fan of Steve Jobs, especially after watching Apple's stock collapse without him. But the yacht he built is truly ugly!"

"Sometimes, not often, but sometimes, less is more." This hardly sounds like a Trump quote, not really brash enough for him, but it shows how he can understand to adapt to the situation. As I studied how he did his business, I began to realise, that as a true master, he can adapt to the situation, to make the best out of it for himself, again similar to Steve Jobs' philosophy and maybe this is why I felt I could follow my best-selling *Jobsology* book with a *Trumpology* book!

Having learnt to respect him, from having studied his business strategies, I feel that he has, particularly recently during the presidential campaign, been badly misrepresented through very biased major media coverage. They focused on any possible negative aspect of him, which in reality is only a very tiny fraction of his repertoire; I feel we must look at every single facet of a person, to truly understand what makes them tick.

Which brings me to the last angle of studying him — the way he talks. The best way to study someone is to study their mottos; they must practice what they preach!! I won't dwell on this too long, as you can now read and enjoy some of my favorite Trump quotes, and decide for yourselves what your opinion about him is. I hope that by reading some of his selected quotes you will be able to see a different side of Trump, compared to that which has been recently spread by the mass media and that his quotes may be as helpful to you as they have been to me.

Cheers,

Chris Chang

　　或許引用另一位大師的格言來做為川語錄的開頭有點奇怪，但我仍要以我相當佩服的 Warrent Buffet 的話：「留在原地，就能完成大部分的事。」來做為開場。

　　為何我這麼做？答案在如下川普的名言：「我不太出門，大多是因為這很浪費時間。」這兩句話聽起來很相似，不是嗎？不只這兩位偉大的企業家共享這信念，連已逝的，偉大的賈伯斯也提過這觀點：「如果你想環遊世界去找老師，他即在你左右。」

　　為何是川普？

　　20 年前，當我從美國念完博士回來，想買下辦公室開始自己的生意，我在沒有

任何房地產經驗的情況下，從我認為最棒的川普尋求建議。在閱讀他的「交易的藝術」，我開始覺得他的生意洞察力啟發了我。當他開始競選美國總統時，我拍掉這書上的灰塵並重讀此書，我看到自己對他的興趣如何地演變，我相信要了解他，不只要研究他的生意經驗，還必須研究他的生活方式，當然，還有他說過的話語。

我從三個角度來研究川普：首先，他生活的方式，尤其是他每天的例行工作；其次，他經營生意的方式；第三則是他說話的方式。

正如你可能知道的，他居住在紐約市最大的閣樓，這毫無意外，因他有「大

手」！他住在 66、67、68 樓，這是最棒的地方來觀賞「大蘋果」。他的辦公室在 26 樓，有著私人電梯直接連接他的住家與辦公室，用餐的餐廳也在這川普大樓內。因此，他大部分的日子都花在這棟大樓，把時間用在他真正的需求上，他日常生活反應出他的習慣，以致於讓他成為一位相當成功的企業家。

　　他經營生意的某些方法很與眾不同，而且是有系統地排序。第一優先是電話，第二是人們可以到他的辦公室來，第三（相當少見）是他去找對方。其中一個我最欣賞的交易，是他有計劃地買下 Mar-a-Lago，這棟當時他被告知絕對不可能買得到的建築。這棟建築在 1973 年被捐給政府

準備當做冬天的白宮。然而，在 1980 年，因維護費用高達美金百萬而又回到原來的主人家手上。有著市場直覺的川普立刻介入，他先買下週邊的土地，再以相當的低價買下主建築。如你對此有興趣，只要上網搜尋「Mar-a-Lago」，你會驚奇川普把它改變成現在如此完美的仙境，這真是不可置信！他是真正的房地產大亨（大師）。

這種不僅想法突破框架，且作法也突破窠臼的行為讓我深深著迷，我覺得這樣的思考方式是他最偉大的資產之一，也證實川普與賈伯斯相似之處，不勝枚舉。川普曾公開地表達他對賈伯斯的敬佩——我一直都是賈伯斯迷，尤其在看到蘋果因沒有他而股市崩盤——但他建造的遊艇真的很醜。

「有時候，並非時常，但有時候，少即是多。」這聽起來不太像川普的話，不夠粗俗，但它展現出川普如何順應環境。當我研究他是如何做生意，我開始了解到，有如真正的大師一般，他能夠適應環境，再善用環境，這也是賈伯斯的哲學，或許也是我覺得我可以接續我最暢銷的**賈語錄**之後，再發行川語錄的原因。

在研究過他的商業策略，因而開始尊敬他之後，我覺得他，尤其是近來在總統選舉時，被相當偏頗的主流媒體嚴重地誤傳，他們專注在塑造任何可能的負面形象，而這只不過是他總體的一小部分。我覺得我們必須看一個人的各個面向來了解為何他能與眾不同。

　　瞭解他的最後一個面向——他說話的
方式。研究一個人最好的方式就是研究他
的格言，因為他們講的一定是他們所做的。
不用我多說，你可以自己閱讀，享受這些
我最喜愛的川語錄，再決定你自己的意見。
我希望你讀了這些選出來的語錄，再去比
較那些主流媒體所散佈的，你能看到川普
不一樣的一面，那麼他的語錄也許會對你，
如同對我一樣，也有所幫助。

　　　　　　　　　　　　張慧男

Chapter One

Personality
人　　格

I rarely go out, because mostly, it's a waste of time.

我不太出門，大多是因為這很浪費時間。

Sometimes — not often, but sometimes —
less is more.

有時候，並非時常，但有時候，少即是多。

Think outside the box and
perform outside the box.

跳脫框架，思考並執行。

Watch, listen, and learn. You can't know it all yourself. Anyone who thinks they do is destined for mediocrity.

觀察、聆聽、然後學習。你不可能全都知道。那些自認為什麼都知道的人註定平庸。

The most important thing in life is to love what you're doing, because that's the only way you'll ever be really good at it.

生命中最重要的事：熱愛你的工作。因為，這是讓你出類拔萃的唯一途徑。

I'm competitive, and I love to create challenges for myself. Maybe that's not always a good thing. It can make life complicated.

我很有競爭力，我也喜歡為自己創造挑戰。
也許這不全是好事，這可以讓人生複雜。

I played golf with my friends, and then I started to play with the hustlers. And I learned a lot. I learned about golf; I learned about gambling. I learned about everything.

我和朋友打高爾夫，後來也和一些皮條客來往，我學到很多，關於高爾夫，關於賭博，關於所有事。

My father was very energetic; my mother was very energetic. He lived to a very old age, and so did my mother. I believe that I just have it from my father, from my parents.

我父母十分生龍活虎，而且都很長壽。我想我有遺傳到他們。

Courage is not the absence of fear. Courage is the ability to act effectively, in spite of fear.

勇氣並非無所懼。而是在懼怕之餘，仍有能力做有效的反應。

Personality Business Politics Joke & Etc.

What separates the winners from the losers is how a person reacts to each new twist of fate.

贏家和輸家的分別，在於對每個命運轉折作出的反應。

When you are wronged repeatedly, the worst thing you can do is continue taking it — fight back!

當你一再被誤解、被不公不義的對待，而你卻一直忍受這是最糟的，反擊吧！

Don't get sidetracked. If you do get sidetracked, get back on track as soon as possible. Ultimately sidetracking kills you.

不要偏離軌道。如果偏離了，要儘快回到正常軌道。無止境的偏離會害死你。

It's always good to be underestimated.

被低估總是好的。

Personality Business Politics Joke & Etc.

People who are capable of thinking for themselves
will rarely be part of any herd.

有獨立思考能力的人，就不會隨波逐流。

Most people think small because they are afraid of success, afraid of making decisions, afraid of winning.

大部分的人不敢太有夢想（小看自己），因為他們害怕成功、害怕決定、並且害怕贏。

Personality Business Politics Joke & Etc.

Creative people don't need to be motivated by
anyone else. They motivate themselves.

有創意的人不需要別人來激勵。
他們自我激勵。

Due diligence equals increasing your
financial IQ daily.

應有的勤奮等同於每天增長你的財務知識。

Do not neglect your life skills, which should include a healthy dose of financial education.

別忽略你的生活技巧，尤其需包含適量的財務教育。

I'm an intuitive person.

我是個第六感很強的人。

Precision, instinct and tempo are all necessary in order to become extraordinary.

準確、直覺、節奏是達到非凡的必要因素。

I like to think of the word FOCUS as Follow One Course Until Successful.

我喜歡將專注（FOCUS）解釋為「遵循一條路線直到成功為止。」

Personality　Business　Politics　Joke & Etc.

Focus is essential to success, and successful
people are people who can focus.

專注為成功之母。那些成功的人都是可以
專注的人。

Keep your focus intact, and focus on the solution.

保持完全的專注，並專注於解法。

Where there's a will, there's a way.

有志者事竟成。

Nothing great in the world has been accomplished without passion.

沒有熱情就無法成就偉大。

Without passion you don't have energy, without energy you have nothing.

沒有熱情就沒有能量，沒有能量等於你一無所有。

Give yourself a little freedom to develop into something or someone you'd actually like to be.

給自己一點空間去發展你實際上想要成為的人或事。

The more you learn, the more you realise how much you don't know.

你學得越多，越能認清自己的不足。

Sheer persistence is the difference between success and failure.

成功和失敗只有一線之隔，就是絕對的堅持。

What matters is where you want to go. Focus in the right direction!

重要的是你想往哪裡走，專注在對的方向。

My motto is: Always get even. When somebody screws you, screw them back in spades.

我的座右銘是：「平等至上。以牙還牙、以眼還眼。」

A little more moderation would be good. Of course, my life hasn't exactly been one of moderation.

再中庸一點或許不錯，不過我人生中絕無模擬兩可的中庸這回事。

The biggest risk we all face is not moving forward with what we've learned.

我們所面臨的最大風險是沒有與我們所學的一同前進。

Personality   Business   Politics   Joke & Etc.

What's the point of having great knowledge and keeping it to yourself?

雖有豐富的知識，卻不分享，
有什麼意義呢？

If something is going to affect your life, it's best to know as much as you can about it.

若有件事即將影響你的人生，最好對它多加了解。

Know everything you can about what you're doing. (by Fred Trump, Donald Trump's father)

要盡全力瞭解你在做的事的所有細節及相關連的事物。（引述自川普父親－佛瑞德·川普）

As long as you are going to be thinking anyway, think big.

反正你得思考，為何不想得遠大點？

Personality   Business   Politics   Joke & Etc.

It doesn't cost anything to dream. Spend your time enjoying your big dreams.

做夢不用花錢，所以花時間享受你的美夢吧。

I've been making deals all my life.

我的一生都在做交易。

Personality Business Politics Joke & Etc.

I have never believed that prosperity is bad or something to be shunned.

我從不相信榮華富貴是不好的，或是要讓人敬而遠之的事。

Trust in God and be true to yourself. (by Mary Anne MacLeod Trump, the mother of Donald Trump)

相信神並對自己誠實。（引述自川普母親—瑪莉‧安‧麥克勞德‧川普）

People are so shocked when they find out I am Protestant. I am Presbyterian. And I go to church, and I love God, and I love my church.

當人們發現我是新教徒時，他們都會非常驚訝。我是長老會者。我去教會聚會，我愛上帝，我也愛教會。

Stay confident even when something bad happens. It is just a bump in the road. It will pass.

即使不好的事情發生仍要保持自信。這不過是路上的坑疤，一切都會過去，如雲煙消逝。

Personality Business Politics Joke & Etc.

A lot of people don't like to win. They actually don't know how to win, and they don't like to win because down deep inside they don't want to win.

很多人不喜歡贏。事實上他們不知道怎麼贏。但他們不喜歡贏主要還是因為他們內心深處並不想贏。

There's an old German proverb to the effect that fear makes the wolf bigger than he is, and that is true.

有句德國古諺說:「恐懼讓野狼變大了。」, 而這是真的。

Personality   Business   Politics   Joke & Etc.

Anyone who thinks my story is anywhere near over is sadly mistaken.

認為我的故事即將結束的人，是大錯特錯。

Owning a great golf course gives you great power.

擁有一個高爾夫球場讓你感覺強大。

Philanthropic efforts are among the best rewards you can have for a life well lived.

慈善事業是你生活最好的獎賞，讓你不虛此生。

Being stubborn is a big part of being a winner.

執著，是成為贏家的重要因素。

Do the right thing right.

把對的事做對。

Always think positively and expect the best.

總要正面思考，並期待最好的。

Don't underestimate yourself or your possibilities.

不要小看你自己，不要低估自己的潛能。

Living your words, walking your talk, and talking your walk.

身體力行，走你所說，說你所走。

Everything in life is luck.

生命中的大小事都是運氣、都是機會。

Be open to new information and ideas.

對新資訊和想法敞開心胸。

Be willing to take on new challenges.

樂於接受新挑戰。

Once you have control, get creative.

當你有掌控權時，有創意些。

Personality Business Politics Joke & Etc.

Use your work to better yourself.

用你所做的使自己更好。

Stand for yourself.

為自己站出來。

Know what you are up against.

知道自己面對什麼。

You have to leave your comfort zone.

你必須離開舒適圈。

Know when to quit.

知道何時退出。

Show me someone without an ego, and I'll show
you a loser.

沒有自我的人就是輸家。

I don't like losers.

我不喜歡輸家。

Luck does not come around often. So when it does, be sure to take full advantage of it, even if it means working very hard. When luck is on your side it is not the time to be modest or timid. It is the time to go for the biggest success you can possibly achieve. That is the true meaning of thinking big.

好運不常有。遇到時就應該善用它,即使這表示必須非常努力。你無需感到謙虛或羞怯,那是你前往更高成就的時機,這就是想得遠大的真正意義!

Business
企　　業

Money was never a big motivation for me, except as a way to keep score. The real excitement is playing the game.

金錢並非激勵我的最大因素，只是衡量分數的方式。遊戲本身才是刺激所在。

If you're interested in 'balancing' work and pleasure, stop trying to balance them. Instead make your work more pleasurable.

停止嘗試在工作與樂趣間取得平衡，而是嘗試將工作做得更有樂趣。

I try to learn from the past, but I plan for the future by focusing exclusively on the present. That's where the fun is.

我嘗試從歷史中學習，但我只專注以當下來規劃未來，這才是樂趣所在。

Vision remains vision until you focus, do the work, and bring it down to earth where it will do some good.

若不專注、實行、在現實中實踐並對人類有所貢獻，眼界就只是眼界而已。

The main job of the entrepreneur is to define the mission, find and inspire the team, and lead.

企業家的主要工作是定義任務，找到、啟發團隊，並領導他們。

To be successful in the world of entrepreneurs, especially in the early stages, a person must learn to fail, correct, learn, apply what was learned, and fail again.

要在企業界成功，尤其在早期，必須學習失敗、修正、學習、並應用所學，然後再度失敗。

A great leader has to be flexible, holding his ground on the major principles but finding room for compromises that can bring people together.

一位優秀的領導者必須處事圓融，堅守主要原則，保留退讓空間來凝聚意識。

Leaders, true leaders, take responsibility for the success of the team, and understand that they must also take responsibility for the failure.

真正的領導者為團隊的成功負責，並也知道他們必須為團隊的失敗負責。

When people are in a focused state, the words I can't, I'll try, I'll do it tomorrow, and maybe get forced out of their vocabularies.

當人們在專注的狀態，那些「我不行」、「我再試試」、「我明天再做」、「可能吧」將會消失在他們的字典裡。

Personality **Business** Politics Joke & Etc.

Part of being a winner is knowing when enough is enough. Sometimes you have to give up the fight and walk away, and move on to something that's more productive.

成為贏家的一部分是知道何時該收手。有時你必須放棄並收手,然後找到更有生產力的事情繼續下去。

The successful entrepreneur's unique ability is to turn trying times into triumphs.

成功企業家的特有能力是將嘗試的次數變為勝利的號角。

I wasn't satisfied just to earn a good living. I was looking to make a statement.

我並不滿足於只是賺錢過好日子，我希望有更大的作為。

Unite to win. Divide to conquer.

團結取勝；分而治之。

Strong relationships are the key.

堅固的人際關係才是關鍵。

People must work together for a company to thrive.

團結合作，公司才能欣欣向榮。

Personality **Business** Politics Joke & Etc.

In business, cooperation is essential to success.

在生意上，合作是成功的關鍵。

Partnerships must have loyalty and integrity at their core.

合夥須以忠誠和正直為核心。

It's next to impossible to build a successful business without relationships.

沒有人際關係，要建立成功事業是幾乎不可能的。

He who has never learned to obey cannot be a
good commander. (by Aristotle)

不知道順服的人沒辦法成為好的指揮官。
（引述自亞里斯多德）

Personality **Business** Politics Joke & Etc.

Beggars can't be choosers.

人在屋簷下，不得不低頭。乞求者是沒得
挑三撿四的。

Rules are meant to be broken.

規則就是用來打破的。

Personality **Business** Politics Joke & Etc.

You can't be imaginative or entrepreneurial if you're got too much structure.

如果你太固守成規，你無法成為有創造性和創業性的人。

The biggest little thing for entrepreneurs is the lifelong commitment to education.

對於企業家最重要的小事就是終生學習。

We've realised the situation will not change so the answer is for us to change.

我們了解到這個情況並不會改變，所以答案應該是我們要改變。（山不轉路轉）

Building a brand may be more important than building a business.

建立品牌比建立事業更重要。

A brand is two words: the 'Promise' you telegraph, and the 'Experience' you deliver.

品牌就是兩個詞：
發出「承諾」，傳遞「體驗」。

Your business, and your brand, must first let people know what you care about, and that you care about them.

你的事業和品牌必須先讓人們知道你所在意的且你在乎他們。

Remember, there's no such thing as an unrealistic goal — just unrealistic time frames.

記住，沒有不切實際的目標，只有不切實際的時間框架。

The worst of times often create the best opportunities to make good deals.

最壞的時機常帶來最好的機會和交易。

Success comes from failure, not from memorizing the right answers.

失敗為成功之母，記住正確答案並不會讓你成功。

Sometimes understanding other people's problems is the key to finding opportunities.

有時候花時間傾聽別人的問題，是你找到機會的關鍵。

I have learned that what is essential can sometimes be invisible to the eye. That's where discernment comes in.

我學到有時候必要的東西會隱藏在檯面下，那就是需要洞察力的時候。

"You will reap what you sow," rings true again. And you will be reaping it. A good thing to think about.

「種瓜得瓜，種豆得豆（你怎麼種，就怎麼收）」再度聽起來是對的。 你會有收穫的，這是個很值得思考的事。

You don't reward failure by promoting those responsible for it, because all you get is more failure.

你不能獎勵那些要為失敗負責的人，這會讓你一敗塗地。

Investors are visionaries in some respects — they look beyond the present.

投資者在某些層面來說是有遠見的，他們並不著眼於當下。

Don't depend on anyone but yourself for providing your financial security.

你應依靠自己而非他人
來確保你的財務安全。

I rely on myself very much. I just think that you have an instinct and you go with it. Especially when it comes to deal-making and buying things.

我很信任自己。我認為要相信你的直覺，特別是在做生意或買東西時。

Personality   **Business**   Politics   Joke & Etc.

My style of deal-making is quite simple and straightforward. I aim very high, and then I just keep pushing and pushing and pushing to get what I'm after.

我做生意的方式很簡單也很直覺。
我訂高目標並且不斷推進再推進，直到得
到我想要的。

As an entrepreneur, I choose my teachers carefully, very carefully. I am extremely cautious of the people with whom I spend my time and to whom I listen.

作為一個企業家，我慎選導師。對於那些我花時間相處的人和提供我意見的人，我總是無比謹慎。

I don't hire a lot of number-crunchers, and I don't trust fancy marketing surveys. I do my own surveys and draw my own conclusions.

我不雇用很多嚼數字的人（精算師），我也不相信花俏的市場調查，我只做我自己的勘查並得出我自己的結論。

I have a very simple rule when it comes to management: hire the best people from your competitors, pay them more than they were earning, and give them bonuses and incentives based on their performance. That's how you build a first-class operation.

我有一些用在管理上的基本原則，從你的競爭對手雇來最優秀的人才，提供他們更優渥的收入，並根據他們的表現給予獎金和激勵，這就是最高級的營運方式。

Experience taught me a few things. One is to listen to your gut, no matter how good something sounds on paper. The second is that you're generally better off sticking with what you know. And the third is that sometimes your best investments are the ones you don't make.

經驗教我幾件事，一、相信你的直覺，不管理論上聽起來多棒，二、盡可能堅持做你所知道的，三、有時候你沒做的投資是最好的投資。

One of the problems when you become successful is that jealousy and envy inevitably follow. There are people — I categorize them as life's losers — who get their sense of accomplishment and achievement from trying to stop others. As far as I'm concerned, if they had any real ability they wouldn't be fighting me, they'd be doing something constructive themselves.

當你成功後會遇到的其中一個問題就是遭忌。那些人——我將他們分類為生命的輸家——是用阻擾他人來獲得讚美和成就。我認為若是他們真有實力，就不會來跟我爭鬥，他們會做其他更有建設性的事。

I have used the laws of this country just like the greatest people that you read about every day in business have used the laws of this country, the chapter laws, to do a great job for my company, for myself, for my employees, for my family, et cetera.

就像你在商業界每天見到的那些大人物一樣，他們運用法律——那些法律章節，我也運用這個國家的法律來為我的公司、我自己、我的員工、我的家庭等等做偉大的工作。

Do not spend too much time planning or trying to anticipate and solve problems before they happen. That is just another kind of excuse for procrastination. Until you start, you won't know where the problems will occur. You won't have the experience to solve them. Instead, get into action, and solve the problems as they arise.

不用花太多時間規劃或試著期待和解決還沒有發生的問題。這只是延遲做事的藉口。在你開始之前，你不會知道問題在哪裡出現，你也不會有解決的經驗。反而，放手去做，當問題出現時再來解決。

I built a great company, one of the — some of the most iconic assets in the world, $10 billion of net worth, more than $10 billion of net worth, and frankly, I had a great time doing it.

我創立了一間很棒的公司，是在世界上最具指標性的資產，淨值百億或更多。老實說，我做得很愉快。

The point is, you can never be too greedy.

重點是，沒有太貪心這件事。

Personality   **Business**   Politics   Joke & Etc.

1962
Works for father's company
Elizabeth Trump and Son.

1946
Born.

196
Gr
Mi

1986
Completes
Wollman Rink.

1983
Grand opening of Tru
Tower in Manhattan.

1985
Purchases
Mar-a-Lago estate.

1987
Trump: The Art of the Deal
is published.

1992
Divorces Ivana.

1990
$900M in debt and
faces bankruptcy.

1992
Three casinos - Taj Mahal,
The Castle, and The Plaza -
go bankrupt.

2007
Opens Trump Place (His biggest
project - 100 acres - on the west side
of Manhattan, which takes 20 years
to finish).

2005
Marries Slovenian mod
Melania Knauss.

2011
Identifies with the
Independent Party.

2009
Grand opening Trump
International Hotel and
Tower in Chicago.

2009
Identifies with the
Republican Party.

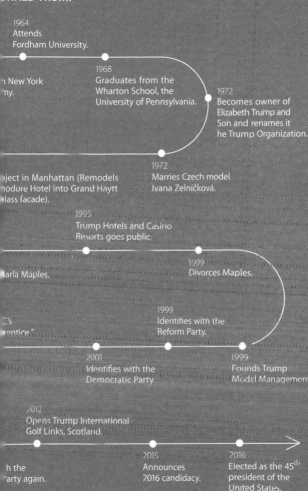

ONALD TRUMP

1964
Attends
Fordham University.

1968
Graduates from the
Wharton School, the
University of Pennsylvania.

n New York
ny.

1972
Becomes owner of
Elizabeth Trump and
Son and renames it
he Trump Organization.

oject in Manhattan (Remodels
modore Hotel into Grand Haytt
lass facade).

1972
Marries Czech model
Ivana Zelníčková.

1995
Trump Hotels and Casino
Resorts goes public.

arla Maples.

1999
Divorces Maples.

C's
rentice"

1999
Identifies with the
Reform Party.

2001
Identifies with the
Democratic Party.

1999
Founds Trump
Model Management

2012
Opens Trump International
Golf Links, Scotland.

h the
arty again.

2015
Announces
2016 candidacy.

2016
Elected as the 45th
president of the
United States.

The more predictable the business, the more valuable it is.

越可以預測的事業越有價值。

And if it can't be fun, what's the point?

若無趣，還有什麼意義？

This is serious business. But it doesn't mean we can't have some fun along the way.

這是個嚴肅的工作，但不代表我們不能從中獲得一些樂趣。

Make every day extraordinary no matter what
your job is.

不管你的工作是什麼，把每一天都變得不
平凡。

You do your job, you keep your job. Do it well, you get a better job.

把事做完，就不會丟掉飯碗；把事做好，你會獲得更好的工作。

The harder you work, the luckier you get.

越努力工作，你會越幸運。

Always try to improve on your performance.

總要試著去改善表現。

Make sure the product is worth your energy.

確保產品值得你的付出。

Thinking expansively includes seeing what is possible and making it happen.

廣泛思考，包含看到事情的可能性並實現。

Brainpower is the ultimate leverage.

腦力是終極手段。

Creativity and control can go hand in hand.

創意和控管可以並行不悖。

I only work with the best.

我只與最頂尖的人工作。

Having the right team is the best form of leverage.

擁有對的團隊是最好的槓桿形式（可創造出最大效益）。

I'm a big free trader, but it has to be fair.

我是自由貿易者，但前提事要公平。

You're fired!

你被解雇了！

I mean, there's no arguing. There is no anything. There is no beating around the bush. 'You're fired' is a very strong term.

沒有任何爭議，不用拐彎抹角，「你被解雇了！」是一個非常強烈的詞。

Well, yes, I've fired a lot of people. Generally I like other people to fire, because it's always a lousy task. But I have fired many people.

是的，我解僱過很多人，一般來說我喜歡讓別人做這件事，因為那是個不討好的任務，但我確實解僱過不少人。

It's a great thing when you can show that you've been successful and that you've made a lot of money and that you've employed a lot of people.

當你可以展現你有多麼成功、多麼富有、和你雇用這麼多人是一件很棒的事。

There's always opposition when you do something big. I do many things that are controversial. When people see it, they love it.

當你做大事時通常都伴隨著反對聲浪。我做了很多有爭議性的事，但當人們看見時，他們也很喜歡。

The way I run my business seems to be easier than the way I run my life.

對我而言，經營事業似乎比經營生活容易。

I don't make deals for the money. I've got much
more than I'll ever need. I do it to do it.

我不是為了錢做生意。我賺的已經多於我
所需要的。我是為了做而做。

I'm passionate about real estate, and that's what works for me.

我熱愛房地產，對我而言，再適合不過了。

It's tangible, it's solid, it's beautiful. It's artistic, from my standpoint, and I just love real estate.

站在我的立場，房地產是有形的，穩固的，美麗的，藝術的，我就是熱愛房地產。

Location, location, location.

地點決定一切。

I'm the No. 1 developer in New York, I'm the biggest in Atlantic City, and maybe we'll keep it that way.

我在紐約是第一名的開發者，在亞特蘭大城市也是最大的，或許我們會繼續保持。

I deal with foreign countries. I made a lot of money dealing against China. I've made a lot of money dealing against many other countries.

我跟很多國家做生意。我和中國做生意賺很多錢，和其他國家做生意也賺不少錢。

The first thing the secretary types is the boss.

身為秘書，第一件事就是要先認清你的老
闆（的類型）。

I have women working in high positions. I was one of the first people to put women in charge of big construction jobs. And, you know, I've had a great relationship with women.

我讓女性居高位。我是第一位讓女性負責大建築案,而且你知道,我也與女性擁有很好的關係。

Politics
政　　　　治

Make America great again.

讓美國再次偉大！

We just want to be strong — and they, the America people, want to be strong again.

我們只是想要堅強。
美國人民想要再次強大。

Drain the swamp.

抽乾沼澤（意指從根本上徹底地改變華盛頓的政治生態）。

Personality   Business   **Politics**   Joke & Etc.

I will not let you down.

我不會讓你們失望。

A tiny leak can sink a ship.

小漏能沉大船；千里之堤毀于蟻穴。

I judge people based on their capability, honesty, and merit.

我根據人的能力、誠實、價值來評論人。

When somebody challenges you, fight back. Be brutal, be tough.

當有人挑戰你時，要頑強地反擊。

Sometimes by losing a battle you find a new way to win the war.

有時輸掉一場戰役，能讓你發現一個新的方法去贏得整場戰事。

In the end, you're measured not by how much you undertake, but by what you finally accomplish.

最終，並非以你所可以承受的，而是以你最後成就的，來評估你這個人。

Criticism is easier to take when you realize that the only people who aren't criticized are those who don't take risks.

當你發現不會被批評的人都是不敢冒險的人時，你就比較容易接受批評。

I want to tell the world community that while we will always put Americas interest first, we will deal with everyone fairly.

我想要跟民眾說當我們總是將美國人的利益擺第一時，我們也要公平的對待每一個人。

America will no longer settle for anything less than the best. We must reclaim our country's destiny and reclaim our bold and daring.

美國不會再為那些不是最好的妥協。我們必須重新宣告我們國家的命運、我們的膽量及勇氣。

We owe her [Hillary Clinton] a major debt of gratitude for her service to our country.

對於她（希拉蕊）為整個國家做出的貢獻，我們欠她一個道謝。

There are no guarantees, but being ready sure beats being taken by surprise.

雖然不保證適用每件事，但是做好準備一定勝過措手不及。

I have made the tough decisions, always with an eye toward the bottom line. Perhaps it's time America was run like a business.

我做了很多艱難的決定，並總是著眼於重點。也許是時候像經營生意般管理美國。

One of the key problems today is that politics is such a disgrace. Good people don't go into government.

今天一個主要的問題就是政治就是恥辱。
好人是不會從政的。

Sometimes you need conflict in order to come up with a solution. Through weakness, oftentimes, you can't make the right sort of settlement, so I'm aggressive, but I also get things done, and in the end, everybody likes me.

有時候，你需要衝突，以得出解決方案。因為軟弱是解決不了問題的，所以我總是具有侵略性的，但我也完成了事情，而且最後，每個人都喜歡我。

The worst things in history have happened when people stop thinking for themselves and listen to other people and, even worse, start following other people. That's what gives rise to dictators.

歷史上曾發生過最糟的事是當人們不再獨立思考而去聽信旁人，更糟的是，開始跟從其他人。這興起了獨裁。

If I were a liberal Democrat, people would say I'm the super genius of all time. The super genius of all time. If you're a conservative Republican, you've got to fight for your life. It's really an amazing thing.

假使我是一個開明的民主黨員，人們會說我是有史以來的超級天才。有史以來的超級天才。但如果你只是一個保守的共和黨員，你就必須爭取你的生活。這是件很奇妙的事。

The debt limits have to come down. The whole world of debt has to be changed as far as this country is concerned. We have to create jobs and we have to create them rapidly because if we don't things are just going to head in a direction that's going to be almost impossible to recover from.

負債限額必須降下來。就這個國家而言，必須改變負債。我們必須創造工作機會，而且要快，因為我們若不趕快，事情將會到達一個將近無法恢復的境界。

I think the big problem this country has is being politically correct. I've been challenged by so many people, and I don't frankly have time for total political correctness. And to be honest with you, this country doesn't have time either.

這個國家有一個很大的問題就是「政治正確」。我被很多人挑戰，坦白說我沒有時間去想「完全的政治正確」。老實說，這個國家也沒有這個時間。

One thing about television, it brings out personality. People are able to watch me in action. They hear my voice and see my eyes. There's nothing I can hide. That's me. Television brings out your flaws, your weaknesses, your strengths, and you truths. The audience either likes you or it doesn't.

電視呈現了一個人的性格。人們可以從電視中看到我的活動，聽到我的聲音，觀察到我的眼神。我沒有任何可隱藏的。這就是我。電視帶出你的缺點、軟弱、力量和你的真話。觀眾不是喜歡你，不然就是不喜歡你。

If you are a little different, or a little outrageous, or if you do things that are bold or controversial, the press is going to write about you.

若你有點不一樣、或有點極端、或你做事很有膽量或有爭議，媒體就會報導你。

I've met some great people that deal with me in the press. I've also met some people that were very dishonorable, frankly.

在新聞界，跟我打過交道的人，有些人很棒，但坦白說也有一些可恥的人。

There they are out there (at each rally) — the crooked media — we have massive crowds, but they will never show it, because Hillary only gets a few hundred and they would have to show that too!!

他們就在那裡（在各種集會中）——扭曲事實的媒體——他們從不表達民眾的聲音，因為希拉蕊只有幾百人，我們的媒體卻因而播報。

I have embraced crying mothers who have lost their children because our politicians put their personal agendas before the national good. I have no patience for injustice, no tolerance for government incompetence, no sympathy for leaders who fail their citizens.

我擁抱了那些流淚的母親們，她們因這些把個人放在國家利益前的執政者而痛失所愛。我無法忍受不正義，無法容忍不適任的政府，更無法同情那些讓人民失望的領導者。

Good publicity is preferable to bad, but from a bottom-line perspective, bad publicity is sometimes better than no publicity at all. Controversy, in short, sells.

好的知名度勝過不好的,總的來說,無論好壞都比沒有任何知名度好。簡而言之,爭議總有人買單。

The problems we face now — poverty and violence at home, war and destruction abroad — will last only as long as we continue relying on the same politicians who created them in the first place.

我們現今所面臨的問題——內有普遍貧窮及暴力，外有戰爭和破壞——而只要我們繼續倚靠那些製造出這些問題的相同政客，這些問題將會永存。

This is a movement not just about me, but millions of millions of people who want to help make America great again. It's a calling to lead this movement and I am humbled.

這不只是關乎我的（社會）運動，而是關乎那些希望美國再度偉大的千千萬萬的人。這是個呼召要來帶領這個（社會）運動，且使我謙遜。

Government will stop listening to people with special interests and start listening to the forgotten people — you, the middle class, the workers!!

政府將不再聽特殊利益團體的話，會開始傾聽那些被遺忘的人——也就是你們，中產階級和工人們！

We need strength, we need energy, we need quickness and we need brain in this country to turn it around.

我們需要力量，我們需要活力，我們需要速度，我們需要智慧，來翻轉這國家。

I don't like soldiers who were captured — I like those who fought and got away!!

我不喜歡那些被擄的士兵，我喜歡那些會攻擊且逃脫的。

The forgotten men and women of our country will be forgotten no longer.

曾經被我們國家忽略的男人與女人們將不再被遺忘。

If people can just pour into the country illegally,
you don't have a country.

若可以非法移民，國家將不復存在。

A certificate of live birth is not the same thing by any stretch of the imagination as a birth certificate.

出生證明在各種層面來說
都跟戶口名簿不同。

I feel a lot of people listen to what I have to say.

我覺得很多人聽我必須得說的話。

People are tired of seeing politicians as all talk and no action.

人們已經厭倦看到政客光說不練。

Politicians can't manage. All they can do is talk.

政客不會管理，他們能做的只是談論。

You don't get a standing ovation and get boos, by the way. They don't go hand in hand.

順道一提，你不會同時得到掌聲和噓聲。

I'm a believer in the polls, by the way. Rarely do you see a poll that's very far off.

我很相信民調，附帶一提，你很少看到民調如此不準。

I've been dealing with politicians all my life. All my life. And I've always gotten them to do what I need them to do.

我一生都在和政客相處，而我總是能讓他們為我做我需要的事。

I shake hands very gladly politically. I don't think you could be a politician if you didn't shake hands.

我樂意於政治上的握手，如果你不握手，我不認為你可以成為政治家。

I have had lobbyists, and I have had some very good ones. They could do anything.

我有一群「說客」，而且有幾位非常優秀，他們可以做任何事。

Personality　　Business　　**Politics**　　Joke & Etc.

I give to everybody. When they call, I give. And do you know what? When I need something from them two years later, three years later, I call them, they are there for me.

我樂善好施。你知道嗎？當我在兩年、三年後尋求他們幫助，他們就在那裡。

I grew up in New York City, a town with different races, religions, and peoples. It breeds tolerance.

我成長於紐約，一個有不同種族、宗教與人民的城市，它孕育著寬容。

My big focus is China and OPEC and all of these countries that are just absolutely destroying the United States.

我將聚焦在中國和 OPEC，還有這些毫無疑問在摧毀美國的國家。

Interesting how the U.S. sells Taiwan billions of dollars of military equipment but I should not accept a congratulatory call from Taiwanese president Tsai Ing-wen.

美國賣十幾億元的武器給台灣，但我卻不能接一通來自臺灣總統蔡英文的祝賀電話，真是有趣！

The pact we have with Japan is interesting. Because if somebody attacks us, Japan does not have to help. If somebody attacks Japan, we have to help Japan.

我們與日本的協定很有趣,如果我們被攻擊,日本不需要幫忙,但如果日本被攻擊,我們一定要幫忙。

Why is it expected to insult and abuse Russia, Why not see if friendship will work??

為什麼要污辱並罷凌俄羅斯，何不嘗試友情是否有用？

Extreme vetting will be normal.

極端審查將會是常態。

Joke & Etc.
笑　　　　　話

I will build a great, great wall on our southern border and I will make Mexico pay for that wall.

我將會在南方邊界建一道巨牆，並讓墨西哥來負擔這筆費用。

Personality   Business   Politics   **Joke & Etc.**

I'm representing them, and they love me and
I love them.

我代表他們，而他們愛我，我也愛他們。

People love me. And you know what, I have been very successful. Everybody loves me.

人們愛戴我。你知道嗎？我很成功。每個人都愛我。

I alone can fix it.

我一人就可搞定！（他隻手就可拯救美國）

Believe me when I say it — believe me!!!

相信我，當我說：「相信我。」

Personality   Business   Politics   **Joke & Etc.**

People assume I'm a boiler ready to explode, but I actually have very low blood pressure, which is shocking to people.

人們說我是隨時沸騰的鍋爐（高血壓），
但其實大家很意外我血壓非常低。

I'm a smart person, I don't need to be told the same thing, by the same people every day. When something changes I am available on the phone within a minute.

我是個聰明人，我不用每天被同樣的一些人重複提醒同樣的事。事情有任何改變時，我可以在電話中馬上處理。

Sorry losers and haters, but my I.Q. is one of the highest, and you all know it! Please don't feel so stupid or insecure, it's not your fault.

全世界都知道我是智商最高的人之一，仇家和輸家們，請不要覺得自己愚蠢或感到不安，這不是你們的錯！

What amazes a lot of people is that I'm sitting in an apartment the likes of which nobody's ever seen. And yet I represent the workers of the world.

使大多數人覺得神奇的是，我坐在一般人從未見過的（豪華）公寓，卻代表著世界上的一般勞工。

You know the funny thing, I don't get along with rich people. I get along with the middle class and the poor people better than I get along with the rich people.

有趣的是，我和富有的人合不來。我跟中產階級和窮人比較處得來。

If they stay in USA and employ American workers then they will pay no tax. If they leave — the goods they send back will be taxed 35% or higher!!!

如果他們（製造業）留在美國並且雇用美國員工，他們將不用繳稅。如果他們離開，他們賣回美國的關稅將會高達 35 % 甚至更多！

I think it's a big scam for a lot of people to make a lot of money — look at China, it's eating our lunch!!!

很多人賺很多錢這件事是個大騙局，看看中國，他們在吃我們的午餐！

When Mexico sends its people, they're not sending their best. They're sending people that have lots of problems, and they're bringing those problems to us. They're bringing drugs. They're bringing crime. They're rapists. And some, I assume, are good people.

當墨西哥輸出他們的人民，他們沒有輸出最好的人。他們送出一堆問題人物，把麻煩丟給我們。他們帶來了毒品、帶來了犯罪，他們是強姦犯。我假設，可能有一些是好人。

We love our companies and we love it when they are employing thousands of people, but we don't love it when they take those jobs and move across the border to Mexico!!

我們愛我們的企業，愛他們雇用上千名員工，但我們不愛他們帶著這些工作和公司跨過墨西哥邊境。

The concept of global warming was created by and for the Chinese in order to make U.S. manufacturing non-competitive.

全球暖化不過是中國製造的謊言，目的是要使美國製造業失去競爭力！

Personality Business Politics Joke & Etc.

Part of the beauty of me is that I am very rich.

我的一部分美麗來自我的富有。

Some people call me lucky, but I know better.

有些人說我幸運，但我知道我更甚於此。

I'm the Ernest Hemingway of 140 characters.

我是140個字的海明威。（我是Twitter天才）

He's lightweight. He is a loser. He is overrated.

他無法勝任，他是失敗者，他被高估了。

Because you'd be in jail.

因為那時你已經進監獄了。

It's freezing and snowing in New York — we need global warming!

紐約這麼寒冷又下雪——
我們需要全球暖化！

Somebody said I am the most popular person in Arizona because I am speaking the truth.

有人說我是亞利桑那州最出名的人，因為我說實話。

I've said if Ivanka weren't my daughter, perhaps I'd be dating her.

我曾說：「如果 Ivanka 不是我女兒，我可能會跟她約會。」

I'm just thinking to myself right now, we should just cancel the election and just give it to Trump, right?

我正在想，我們應該取消選舉，直接宣告川普當選，對吧？

Perhaps I shouldn't campaign at all, I'll just, you know, I'll ride it right into the White House.

或許我根本不需競選，我只要，你知道的，直接進入白宮。

I wouldn't mind a little bow. In Japan, they bow.
I love it. Only thing I love about Japan.

我不介意輕微的鞠躬,在日本,他們鞠躬,
我喜歡,那是日本文化中我唯一喜歡的部分。

Our young people are flying planes so old that when they break down, they need to get spare parts from the museum because they don't make spare part for these planes anymore!!!

我們的年輕人駕駛著古老的機型，因為太舊了，當他們壞掉的時候，他們必須從博物館取得零件，因為這些零件根本已經停產。

We don't want to sit around and talk about attacking ISIS, what we will do, when we will do it, and give them 3 weeks notice to all run away!!! We will build a solid plan and just do it.

我們不會到處閒聊攻擊 ISIS 的事，當我們要做的時候，我們會擬定固若金湯的計畫，並給他們三週的時間逃亡。

We will halt all Islamic immigration from high risk countries until we work out what's going on.

我們將會停止所有來自高風險國家的伊斯蘭移民直到我們可以解決已發生的問題。

I've always said, 'If you need Viagra, you're probably with the wrong girl.'

我總說：「如果你需要威爾鋼（壯陽藥），你可能是選錯女友。」

I think the only difference between me and the other candidates is that I'm more honest and my women are more beautiful.

我與其他候選人唯一的不同，就是我比較誠實，而我的女人比他們的更加美麗。

All of the women on "The Apprentice" flirted with me — consciously or unconsciously. That's to be expected.

不意外地，所有在「誰是接班人」節目上的女性都向我調情，無論是有意還是無意的。

Look at those hands, are they small hands? And he [Rubio] referred to my hands, 'if they're small something else must be small.' I guarantee you there's no problem, I guarantee it.

看看我的手，他們很小嗎？Rubio 指著我的手說：如果他們很小，其他地方也很小。我跟你們保證沒問題的，我保證。

I'll drink water. Sometimes tomato juice, which I like. Sometimes orange juice, which I like. I'll drink different things. But the Coke or Pepsi boosts you up a little.

我喝水，有時喝我喜歡的番茄汁，有時是我喜歡的柳橙汁。我喜歡喝不同的飲料。但可樂或百事可樂比較能提神。

As everybody knows, but the haters & losers refuse to acknowledge, I do not wear a "wig." My hair may not be perfect but it's mine.

如大家所知，那些仇家和輸家拒絕承認，我並不戴「假髮」，我的頭髮縱然不完美但它仍屬於我的。

I have never seen a thin person drinking Diet Coke.

我從來沒有看過一個瘦子喝健怡可樂。

I've always been a fan of Steve Jobs, especially after watching Apple stock collapse without him — but the yacht he built is truly ugly.

我一直都是賈柏斯迷，尤其在看到蘋果因沒有他而股市崩盤——但他建造的遊艇真的很醜。

My Father's Dream
An Interview by Chris' Daughter

張慧男醫師女兒訪談爸爸的夢想

Q1 : What was your childhood dream?

A : To become a painter.

Q2 : Why did you have such a dream?

A : My interest was awoken when I started painting in elementary school.

Q3 : Have you achieved this dream?

A : I later gave up on it.

Q4 : Why?

A : Your grandfather wanted me to do well in school.

Q5 : Did you have any other dreams?

A : Yes.

Q6 : What was your second dream?

A : To become an Orthodontist.

Q7 : Why did you have this dream?

A : After having been accepted in to dental school, my interest in everything related to Orthodontics just grew and grew.

Q8 : Have you achieved your dream?

A : Yes, I have.

My dad fell in love with frog fishing in the summer when he turned 6. This hobby has taught him a valuable lesson: it doesn't take magic power to climb the highest mountain but basic, solid steps. Whatever you do, don't settle for merely getting by, but practice until perfect. After learning this lesson, my dad got closer to his dream.

When he started to catch frogs, he kept refining his frog catching methods; soon after he was able to catch about 100 frogs daily. The real challenge was what to do with all those frogs? How could he put them in a coma, gut them, and then prepare them for food afterward? My dad consulted many people and finally came to his own conclusion. He put them in a plastic bag and shook it well to make the frogs panic. The frogs' bellies would inflate as they breathed in oxygen and breathed out carbon dioxide before they passed out. The inflated belly made it easier to be dissected and gutted. This technique of dissecting frogs proved to be very useful later in his dental school's anatomy lab.

After graduating from primary school, my grandfather enrolled my dad in a private school with the hope that he would excel academically. Coincidentally my dad joined an art club. Compared to his peers he was very talented and won many awards. From dawn to dusk he never went without his paintbrush. Frog-fishing taught him that practice makes perfect and that's what he did. He kept trying to become better at painting and found so much joy in the process. To him, painting was his talent and interest. However, my grandfather didn't see a promising future in painting and my father didn't want to waste the hard-earned money that my grandfather had given him for school. So he gave up painting and focused on school.

When it was time to choose universities, my dad chose to study in the government funded dental program. Back then, it wasn't a popular choice for college education and that's mainly how he got into the program. As a freshman, he knew nothing about dentistry and had to start from the basics. As he invested more hours in it, he began to fall in love with everything related to dentistry. With that and the frog-dissecting skills, he was able to excel at school. Becoming a dentist turned into his second dream. After graduation, my grandparents took their life-savings to support my father's graduate studies overseas where he acquired a more in-depth education about Orthodontics. When he returned to Taiwan, he began his career as a small town Orthodontist. Now he runs his own practice. To many their dream is a job to make a living. However, for my dad being an Orthodontist is not just about making money but sharing his true passion about Orthodontics with others. Now with the opportunities to lecture about Orthodontics around the world, the pleasure of sharing his work makes his job not tough at all.

People's dreams change over time. What

happened in your childhood may have a lasting impact on your life. In the end, the most important question of all is, have you achieved your dreams?

Kristina Chang
(13 years old)

Q：夢想是什麼？
A：當畫家。

Q：為何有這個夢想？
A：國一時接觸畫畫後，對畫畫很感興趣。

Q：是否完成這個夢想？
A：後來放棄這個夢想。

Q：為何要放棄？
A：你阿公希望我能努力讀書。

Q：後來是否還有過其他夢想？
A：有。

Q：第二個夢想是什麼？
A：當牙齒矯正醫師。

Q：為何有這個夢想？
A：考上了牙醫後，學著學著便喜歡上和牙醫矯正有關的事。

Q：是否完成這個夢想？
A：有。

　　我爸爸，在六歲那年的暑假，愛上了釣青蛙，釣青蛙這件事讓他學到了一件寶貴的事：登上世界高峰，不是靠奇招，而是精純熟練的基本功。做什麼事，不只是會就好，而要不斷的練習。學會了這件事，讓爸爸離他的夢想能更近一步。

　　六歲那年暑假，爸爸開始到田裡釣青蛙。每天都在尋找能釣到更多青蛙的方法，

不斷的努力，不久後便能在一天內釣到上
百隻青蛙。但釣到青蛙後，難的在後面，
要如何麻醉上百隻青蛙，並解剖牠，把內
臟都清出來，最後再煮成青蛙湯呢？爸爸
去請教了很多人，最後的結論是：把青蛙
都放進塑膠袋中，再搖一搖，讓青蛙們一
直吸氧氣，一直吐二氧化碳，肚子便會鼓
起來，最後就會暈過去。再來，就是要解
剖青蛙了，肚子鼓起來後，皮會變得緊繃，
會比較好解剖。經過不斷的解剖，讓爸爸
在小學時，就把後來當牙醫要學的解剖都
練得很純熟了。

　　小學畢業後，阿公不再讓爸爸釣青蛙，
把他送到私立學校希望他能好好讀書。

　　沒想到，初一時因緣際會進了美術社，當時在同學中，他的畫畫天分比其他人好，比賽時常常得獎。那時從早到晚，畫筆從不離手，從青蛙的事件中讓爸爸學會要不斷的練習。所以他每天不停的練習畫畫，努力的想畫的更好。他覺得畫畫是件有趣的事，畫畫就是他的興趣和專長。但是，阿公並不認為畫畫有什麼前途，我爸爸不想讓阿公辛苦賺給他讀書的錢浪費掉，便放棄了畫畫，開始努力讀書。

　　到了要考大學，因為家裡沒多少錢，爸爸便決定去考不用繳學費的國防牙醫系。當時牙醫並不熱門，爸爸就這樣考上了牙醫系。考上了牙醫系後，爸爸什麼都不懂，只能從頭學起，但學著學著，便開

始愛上了有關牙醫的一切，加上小時候的
解剖訓練，讓爸爸在牙醫方面有比其他人
更上一層樓。當牙醫便是爸爸的第二個夢
想。畢業後，阿公阿嬤拿出家裡的積蓄讓
爸爸出國唸書。在國外爸爸學到更多和牙
醫有關的東西。回國後，從小矯正牙醫開
始當起，到現在爸爸開了屬於自己的矯正
牙醫診所。

爸爸從小到現在，有過的夢想不只兩
個，但當矯正牙醫才是他最終的夢想。現
在矯正牙醫已不再是夢想，爸爸已經實現
了夢想，也開了自己的矯正牙醫診所。很
多人的夢想是能有個工作賺錢，但對爸爸
來說，當矯正牙醫不只是因為要賺錢，而
是他自己喜愛他的工作，將他的矯正牙醫

經驗分享給他人。現在他能有機會到全世界演講矯正牙醫經驗，讓他一點都不覺得當矯正牙醫賺錢很辛苦，而是能快樂的與他人分享。

　　人的夢想會隨著時間而改變，而小時候發生的事也能影響你的一生，但最重要的是，到了最後，你是否曾完成過你的夢想。

張譯文
（13歲）

川語錄
TRUMPology

TRUMP.ology

川語錄

編者	・張慧男
發行人	・張慧男
執行總編輯	・余承勳
責任編輯	・蔡佳汶、朱央如、詹雅婷
英文編輯	・Paul Head
編輯企畫	・陳振芳、張慧中、張慧安、高淑芬
行銷企劃	・蔡佳汶、黃登鍵、朱央如、呂玟縈
封面設計	・張譯文、張瑜珍、余承勳、詹雅婷
美術設計	・Luis Bolumar、黃懍慧、陳建名

Chief Editor	・Chris Chang
Publisher	・Chris Chang
Executive Editor	・Chester Yu
Associate Editor	・Michelle Tsai, Bella Chu, Yuyu Jhan
English Editor	・Paul Head
Planning Editor	・Jenn Fang Chen, Huei Jhong Chang, Hueih An Jang, Shufen Kao
Marketing	・Michelle Tsai, Fancy Huang, Bella Chu, Winnie Lu
Cover Designer	・Kristine Chang, Jenny Chang, Chester Yu, Yuyu Jhan
Art Designer	・Luis Bolumar, Connie Huang, Michael Chen

出版社 · 金牛頓藝術科技股份有限公司

新竹市建中一路 25 號 2 樓

Newton' s A Co., Ltd.

2F., No.25, Jianzhong 1st Rd., Hsinchu City, Taiwan

Tel　　· 886-3-573-5676

Fax　　· 886-3-573-6777

E-mail · info@newtonsa.com.tw

印刷 · 鴻順印刷文化事業（股）公司

Printed and bound in Taiwan

by Hopeson Color Printing co., Ltd.

定價 · 260 元 | 2017 年 1 月 20 日初版

List Price · US$8 | First published on Jan 20, 2017

ISBN 978-986-88779-2-4

Must Read: Jobsology 賈語錄

賈語錄

Jobsology

The Wisdom of **Steve Jobs**

SECOND EDITION 第二版

讓您受用一生的賈伯斯精簡名句

Chris Chang

Newton's A 金牛頓藝術科技
+886-3-5735676 info@newtonsa.com.tw